HANDYMAN'S LITTLE BOOK OF WISDOM

By Bob Algozzine

ICS BOOKS, Inc.
Merrillville, IN

Handyman's Little Book of Wisdom
Copyright © 1996 by Bob Algozzine
10 9 8 7 6 5 4 3 2 1

All inquiries should be addressed to ICS Books, Inc., 1370 E. 86th Place, Merrillville, IN 46410

Published by: **Printed in the U.S.A.**   Co-Published in Canada by:
ICS BOOKS, Inc.   Vanwell Publishing LTD
1370 E. 86th Place   Cover illustrations by   1 Northrup Crescent
Merrillville, IN 46410   Demetrius Saulsberry   St. Catharines, Ontario
800-541-7323   L2M 6P5
                                                             800-661-6136

Library of Congress Cataloging-in-Publication Data

Algozzine, Robert
      Handyman's little book of wisdom / by Bob Algozzine.
      p.   cm. -- (Little book of wisdom)
      ISBN 1-57034-046-3
1. Repairing--Amateurs ' manuals . 2. Dwellings Maintenance and repair-- Amateurs' manuals.
                  I. Title. II Series .
                  TT151.A43 1996
                  643' .7--dc20   96-22510
                                                   CIP

Dedication

For my dad who taught me that perfect strangers can soon be very close friends, that everything we ever needed was made by somebody just like us, and that being known for what you do is better than you just knowing what to do.

Preface

Many of these bits of wisdom are not original--no telling where they first appeared or who first passed them on to others--maybe like most of the originals, "necessity was the mother of invention," and, conversation was the best way to "pass it on." Thanks to grandparents, parents, brothers and sisters, sons and daughters, uncles, aunts, and all those others who always took the time to share what they knew and sometimes the energy to write them down so backyard handywork became a lot easier.

The goal here is not to share new ideas. Oh, I'm smart enough to have new ideas, but so are you. The problem here is related more to memory than creation. Most of us can't remember all we know. We need to be reminded of some good ideas, now and then. This collection is a reminder.

1.   Measure twice, cut once.

2.   A covering of baking soda overnight
       does a good job on cleaning oil and
       grease from a garage floor.

3.   Tack an old belt on the edge of a shelf
       to use as a tool holder.

4.   Use the striking edge on an old wooden matchbox as a sharpener for pocketknives and other small cutting tools.

5.   Have the right tools, not all the tools.

6. Put putty, wood filler, wall spackle, and other quick drying materials in sealed plastic bags to reduce chances of exposure to outside air ruining them.

7.   Put a duct tape handle on the end of plastic squeeze tubes of caulking or cement and hang them instead of tossing them in a box.

8.   Install viewers in all entry doors.

9.   Keep a journal of all those great places
      you hide things.

10.   Add some hooks to the backs of doors
      to gain some easy storage space.

11.   Clean cat litter is a good closet
      dehumidifier.

12.   Take your time.

13.   A couple charcoal briquettes in a bowl
      will absorb moisture under a sink or in
      a closet.

14. Store garden tools with sharp tongs, tips, or blades facing the wall.

15. To remove mildew, dip the soiled item in buttermilk and lay it in the sun.

16. A spray painted piece of wax paper is not a good replacement for a broken brake light.

17. Wear eye protection when
     working with all power tools.

18. Baking soda wiped on the windshield with a rain-soaked cloth keeps the view clear.

19. To keep mushrooms fresh longer, store them in brown bags not original shrink-wrapped packages.

20. Before making coffee, sprinkle vanilla, peppermint, or other flavoring on grounds to get that frugal gourmet flavor.

21. Pop more holes in a leaky garden hose and turn it into a substitute for an expensive "soaker."

22. Store cut flowers in a raw potato to keep them fresh longer.

23.   Use epoxy putty to repair broken handles on tools--it is easy to shape, but dries hard as a rock.

24.   Pulling works better than pushing with most wrenches.

25. Tapping lightly on a wrench handle works better than sustained pulling for loosening tough nuts.

26. Sawdust mixed with glue makes a great wood filler.

27. A sponge of salt water wiped dry will reduce frost on windows during winter.

28. Masking tape makes a great temporary weatherstripping.

29. Use labels to eliminate memory in emergencies.

30. Store string balls in jars and punch a hole in the top to make dispensing easier.

31. A three-panel screen folded into a U-shape with a broom handle across the top makes a great emergency closet.

32. Duct tape does not make a real good belt.

33. Have a good time.

34. Glossy white enamel paint will make closets brighter.

35. Use a blackboard eraser to smooth wrinkles out of stick-on shelf paper and drawer liners.

36.   A piece of chamois is great for cleaning mist and grime from the inside of your windshield.

37.   Alternatively stack bricks and shelving boards to create designer storage units.

38. Tape a line level on top of your electric
     drill to modernize it and help make
     straight holes.

39. To save on cleanup, tape a coffee filter
     or small paper bag on the wall under
     the spot where you are going to drill a
     hole.

40. Plastic milk cartons cut in appropriate shapes and secured to a wall make great tool holders; keep the caps on and use them to store small parts.

41.   Use golf tees to fill worn or loose screw holes.

42.   Put a tennis ball on the head of your nail hammer to make a mar-proof mallet.

43. Put a couple of medium-size fishing weights in the bottom of your paint cans and use them to agitate and stir the paint before using it.

44.   Toilet seats don't make real good picture frames.

45.   Put some nail holes in the sealing rim of your paint cans to prevent them from filling up when cleaning excess paint from the brush.

46. Nail a section of an old steel tape measure to the side of your sawhorse to use as a quick tool for rough cutting lumber or shelving.

47.   Put 1 x 4 shelves between open studs in your garage or workshop for easy storage of small items.

48.   Use discarded muffin tins covered with thin sheets of plexiglas for storing nuts, bolts, nails, and other small materials.

49. As a prevention measure, use a liquid drain cleaner when you "spring forward" or "fall back" with your clocks.

50. Used auto parts are not a great base for your mailbox.

51. Change heating/air conditioning system filters every month.

52. Plant hangers that swivel make it easier to water plants and rotate all sides toward sunlight.

53. Put labels for tools that store on wall hanging brackets to keep everything in the right place.

54. To save on cleanup, hold a damp washcloth against the wall under the spot where you are going to drill a hole.

55. Don't bother putting wax on a no-wax floor.

56. Don't waste money on high octane gas if you don't need it.

57. Be careful if you use the little blade on your pocketknife when you need to clean your ears or pick your teeth.

58. Fill a cardboard box with scraps
     of large diameter PVC pipe and
     use it to store molding, pipe,
     dowels, and other similar
     materials.

59. Cut the tops off plastic milk cartons and fit them into a cardboard box frame for more small parts storage.

60. Cut the bottom off a plastic milk carton and use it as a dust pan.

61. Use slip-resistant paint on concrete stairs.

62. Salt or a spray of vinegar and water (1:1) will slow slugs.

63. Locking-grip pliers are useful in removing ruined screws.

64. Keep refrigerator coils free of dust to increase efficiency.

65. Uncooked spaghetti makes a nice long "match."

66. Use binder clips available at stationery stores to hang work plans, gloves, and other easily misplaced items.

67. Panty hose and duct tape are not good for towing cars.

68. Things that are easy to do are easy not to do--have a plan.

69. Should, could, will; will change your life--should, could, won't; won't.

70. Don't spend major time on minor things.

71.   Drill holes in a yardstick and use it with one end pivoting when you need a compass for measuring large circles or curves.

72.   Use a blackboard eraser to wipe moisture from any kind of glass.

73. A small scrap of carpet makes a nice grease scrubber for cleaning.

74. Sprinkle cat litter in the bottom of garbage cans to reduce odors; change it whenever it gets wet.

75. Make a border holder for bedding plants from a scrap of guttering capped on both ends.

76. Use bungee cords to keep the tops on garbage cans and other large containers.

77. Buckle up on every car ride.

78. Glue a small magnet to the side of a hammer's head and use it for quick starting nails in high places or small tacks anywhere.

79. Use a rubber wedge-shaped doorstop or scrap of wood to make pulling nails easier.

80. Glue a piece of weatherstripping or a small scrap of leather to the top of your hammer to reduce surface marring when pulling nails.

81. Glue a small magnet to the bottom of a hammer's handle and use it to pick up loose nails and other small parts.

82. Wrap a scrap of bicycle inner tube around screwdriver handles for a better grip.

83. For most screws and fasteners, "Right is Tight" and "Left is Loose."

84.　Slit a scrap of old garden hose and slip it over a saw blade to protect it.

85.　Laundry prewash makes cleaning hands a bit easier.

86. Sawdust and liquid detergent scours hands clean.

87. Dust rubber gloves with talcum powder to make them easier to put on and take off.

88. Learn from negatives as well as positives.

89. Learn by observing; watch and
    pay attention.

90. Work harder on yourself than you do on your job.

91. Wear eye protection.

92. New plastic garbage cans make great attic storage bins; a bar of soap or a few fabric softener sheets gives them a nice smell.

93. Cut the fingers out of old gloves and use them as tool holders.

94. A paste of cream of tartar and water will remove rust from clothes if you wash them after the paste has dried.

95. Put an iron-on patch on the bottom of your pockets to make them last longer.

96. Drill a hole from your workbench top into the front of each drawer and drop a nail or bolt into it to make an easy, child-proof lock.

97. Check smoke detectors and other safety equipment each time you "spring forward" or "fall back" with your clocks.

98. Put a cut-to-fit broom handle in your sliding door track to make it more secure.

99.   Fit a piece of molding over your sliding glass door to make up and down movement more difficult.

100.   Install dead bolts in all entry doors.

101.   Tack some carpet scraps around the main beam of sawhorses to soften the surface.

102. Tape the ends of a manila folder for use in storing sandpaper disks or sheets.

103. Paint thinner sprayed on a saw blade will do a good job of cleaning sticky wood deposits.

104. To store razor blades, safely, put them in matchbooks or aspirin tins.

105. Cross-slit an old tennis ball and use it as a cap to protect the end of small flashlights or tools.

106. Remember--you can't be too
organized.

107. Store glue containers upside down to make application quicker.

108. Store rolls of tape in a plastic bag to make them easier to find and less likely to pick up dirt or become sticky.

109. Use a screen door handle or towel bar as a grip on the side of a wood step ladder.

110. Drill a few holes in the steps of a ladder to use as a place to store tools; use a wall broom holder for your hammer.

111.   Blunt the point of a nail to prevent
        wood splitting.

112.   It's not a good idea to use your mailbox
        to hang up one end of your clothesline.

113.   Check smoke detector batteries every
        month.

114. Saw through a bar of soap to prevent wood deposits from collecting on a saw blade.

115. Cut the fingertips from an old pair of leather gloves and put them over the jaws of your pliers to soften the grip.

116. Slip a bike handlegrip over the end of an adjustable wrench to give it a better grip.

117. Put a furniture leg tip on the end of a hammer to make a softer mallet.

118.   Keep household cleaners, medicines, and power tools out of reach of children.

119.   Keep a first aid kit in your garage, work area, and workshop.

120.   A blown tire is not a good planter for the front porch.

121. Wipe a No. 2 pencil along the sides of a door key and then use it to "lubricate" the lock.

122. Cut a piece of sandpaper to fit on a shoe shine rag and use it to trim a tight-fitting door.

123. Fill loose-fitting screwholes with toothpicks, wooden matchsticks, or golf tees and reset the screws.

124. Start at the bottom when removing doors from hinges.

125. Add some outdoor weatherstripping to interior doors to make them more soundproof.

126. Shape an old broom handle and stick it in a hollow rung of your ladder to use as a paint can holder.

127. Make a tray from a scrap of guttering and two end caps and tack it to the side of a saw horse for storing small tools, nails, and fasteners.

128. The word after "Size" on the Pampers box does not mean how much they will hold.

129. Super strong leftover tea makes a good window and mirror cleaner.

130. A blackboard eraser and crumpled newspaper make great final wipes when cleaning windows.

131. Automatic dishwasher liquid
does a great job on windows
and other household glass.

132. Clean windows on a cloudy day to prevent cleaning agents from drying too fast in the sun.

133. Slip a scrap of old garden hose over an open end wrench to give it a better grip.

134. Put screen molding around the top step of a ladder to corral small parts and tools.

135. Tack an old belt to the wall and use it to keep ladders and other tall equipment secure.

136. Use a drop of hot glue to patch a hole in a plastic bucket.

137. A scrap of tongue and groove lumber makes a great sanding block for tough-to-fit surfaces.

138. Wear rubber gloves when working with glass.

139. Candles or a bar of soap make decent lubricants on sticky windows.

140. Shaving cream makes a good carpet spot remover.

141. Cornmeal, talcum powder, or baking soda can be used to "lift" stains from carpet; just cover the stain and vacuum up the next day.

142. Keep your garbage disposer smelling clean by grinding orange, grapefruit, lemon, or lime peels in it.

143. A spray of vinegar or liquid laundry bleach removes mildew from most surfaces.

144. Remember--you can't have too much storage.

145. A wood plane or chisel can be used for an emergency pencil sharpener.

146. Petroleum jelly on your hands makes cleanup easier after painting.

147. A short soak in a vinegar and water (50:50) solution will soften a brush stiffened with latex paint.

148. Clean cat litter removes odors from closed areas in a couple of days.

149. A mixture of borax and flour (2:1) really bugs roaches (use with caution around children and pets).

150. A few moth balls in the bottom of garbage cans keep flies flocking elsewhere.

151. Store cleaning supplies in plastic buckets to control clutter and make using them "on-the-job" easier.

152. Find nuts to fit each socket in a wrench set and glue them to a board or box to make storage easier.

153. A little baking soda inside rubber gloves makes them easier to put on.

154. Flush a pot of boiling water and equal parts of salt and baking soda down a sluggish drain.

155. A baking soda paste does a good job removing black heel marks from vinyl floors.

156. Use an old toothbrush to clean grime from can openers.

157. Boil baking soda in half a pot of water to help remove scorched material from the bottom.

158. Use stainless-steel or hot-dipped galvanized fasteners outdoors to reduce problems with rusting.

159. Remove the base of a broken light by grabbing the edge with needle-nose pliers and bending it inward to make a "handle" to use in twisting it out (be sure to turn off the power, first).

160. It's not a good idea to paint ceramic tile.

161. Wrap masking tape, sticky side out, around your hand to remove stray fuzz from a paint roller before using it.

162. Yellow glue "sets up" more quickly than white glue.

163. Using an electronic stud locator is an inexpensive way to prevent frustration.

164. An electric razor makes a good substitute for an electronic stud locator.

165. Use a professional-grade
squeegee and <u>a little moisture</u>
to get windows really clean.

166. Vinegar and water will remove lime deposits from teapots; boil and allow mixture to stand overnight.

167.   A towel makes a good cushion when washing fragile items in a porcelain sink.

168.   Coffee, tea, and cigarette stains can be removed by rubbing with a damp cloth dipped in baking soda.

169. Store drills and other small
power tools in plastic lunch
boxes.

170. Store drill bits in an old plastic flashlight or unused eyeglasses container.

171. Spray furniture wax on saw blades and other metal tools to prevent rusting.

172. Place a rubber band around a yardstick for a sliding rule marker.

173. Wrap a piece of tape around a
      pencil leaving a flap to prevent
      it from rolling.

174. Clean and save a few spray
     paint nozzles as replacements
     for a clogged or defective one
     you are trying to use.

175. A wire kitchen whisk makes a great mixer for wet or dry chemicals.

176. Line a plastic cup with a heavy duty freezer bag and use it for an easy cleanup mixing container.

177. Cover cooking pans in
aluminum foil to make
barbecue cleanup easier.

178. Pouring powders into water usually prevents lumps more than pouring water into powder.

179. Put cedar shavings used to fill pet beds in lunch bags, staple the tops shut, and punch a few escape holes to make great fresheners for closets, drawers, and storage chests.

180. Shade and inadequate circulation are ideal conditions for mildew.

181. Pushing heavy objects is usually easier than pulling them.

182. Disassembling an item
      sometimes makes it easier
      to discard.

183. A paste of scouring powder that contains bleach will make mildew removal easier if it stands for a couple hours before you scrub it off.

184. A cup holds 8 ounces, a pint is 2 cups, a quart is 2 pints, a gallon is 4 quarts.

185. Alcohol is a reasonable insecticide for Japanese beetles.

186. A wet tea bag is a good compress for quick relief on an itch.

187. Double-check your math.

188. A beer can opener makes a good grout remover.

189. Old socks make great disposable gloves for messy outside work.

190. Rolling sore feet over a tennis ball can be very refreshing.

191. Tuck fabric softener sheets in your shoes when you're not wearing them.

192. Hardwoods make a hotter, cleaner fire than softwoods.

193. Tears clear small eye irritants better than rubbing.

194. Toothpaste is good for removing crayon marks.

195. Club soda, window cleaner, baking soda, white vinegar or lemon peels do a good job cleaning chrome.

196. A spray of rubbing alcohol will kill most flying insects.

197. Bleach and soapy water make a great mildew remover.

198. Old shingles don't always have to be removed when doing a new roof.

199. Gingersnaps help reduce
motion sickness.

200. Use a Polaroid camera to make a record of complex wiring before disassembling it for repairs.

201. Systemic pesticides are taken in by plants and ingested by insects when they eat leaves or suck on the stem.

202. Non-systemic pesticides are not absorbed by plants but are ingested by insects when they eat leaves or the stem.

203. Contact pesticides kill when they touch insects.

204. Selective pesticides are designed only to kill certain insects or weeds.

205. Non-selective pesticides are not designed to kill certain things; they kill whatever they touch.

206. Nails or nail holes in baseboards or molding can help locate wall studs.

207. Sounds are duller over studding.

208. Wall plugs, light switches, and other electrical contacts are usually attached to wall studs.

209. To prevent wood from splitting, use a pilot hole.

210. Don't drink and drive (nails, a lawnmower, or your car--ouch!).

211. Use shoe polish for small finishing repairs on picture frames, doors, and furniture.

212. A bright colored rag is not a good substitute for a lost gas cap.

213. A trash bag is not a good replacement for a broken window in your car.

214. Used plastic pill bottles or 35mm film containers make great holders for nails and other fasteners.

215. Old ice cube trays and muffin tins make great storage bins for screws, nails, and other small parts.

216. Run screws into and out of a bar of soap to make them insert easier into wood.

217. Tack bungee cords horizontally on a wall for great standup storage racks.

218. Tack small cans on the edge of your workbench to hold tools; remove both ends to hold long handles (hammers) or stack one double open on top of one with a bottom for long tools (screwdrivers).

219. Kerosene (2 parts) combined with lightweight motor oil (one part) is a good solution for removing rust.

220. Use carpet padding or carpet scraps to make tool drawers quieter.

221. Tack a couple of used bicycle inner tubes to the garage wall for storing molding and loose light lumber.

222. Sawdust mixed with thinned nail polish makes a good wood filler.

223. Toothpicks, match sticks, golf tees, and dowels make great mistake fillers.

224. Burn the ends of nylon rope to prevent fraying.

225. Wipe shower curtains and walls with baking soda on a damp sponge to remove mildew.

226. A paste of lemon juice and baking soda works great for cleaning copper.

227. Hot water helps in removing tight bottle and jar caps.

228. Cut the bottom off a plastic milk jug to make a great scoop for filling your bird feeders.

229. Talcum powder, cream of tartar, borax, powdered sulfur, and mint are good ant repellents.

230. Store string balls in cut-off plastic milk jugs and pull string out of a hole in the bottom.

231. Wire two berry baskets together to form another great string dispenser.

232. Coat your hands with petroleum jelly to prevent dirt from soaking in and make cleanup easier.

233. Flushing a hairbrush down the toilet won't clean the pipes real good.

234. Flushing a cup of baking soda down the toilet will help clean a septic tank.

235. There's more than one way to do anything right.

236. Spray furniture polish on a potholder mitt to avoid leaving fingerprints.

237. Shake some uncooked rice, dishwashing liquid, and water in containers with tough-to-clean shapes.

238. To clean silk flowers, shake them in a brown paper bag with some salt.

239. Freezing candle wax and gum makes them easier to remove.

240. "Wash" a gallon of vinegar in hot water to clean your washing machine and dishwasher.

241. Unused batteries last longer if you store them in the refrigerator.

242. Always use a metal bucket to transport fireplace ashes.

243. Light colored paint makes a room look larger.

244. Spray the bottoms of metal trash cans with rust-preventing paint.

245. A garage sale is a great alternative to finding more storage space.

246. A mixture of castor oil (1/2 cup) and water (2 gallons) makes a good mole repellent.

247. Powdered chalk scattered
around garden plants is a good
repellent for ants and slugs.

248. Diluted chlorine bleach can be used to remove odors from coolers and other closed containers.

249. Automatic dishwashing detergent makes a great outdoor window cleaner.

250. Newspapers make great mulch--poke a few holes in them and cover with dirt.

251. Start your mower with fresh gas each new season.

252. Paint the handles of garden tools in a bright color so they are easier to spot when left in the yard.

253. Plastic packing peanuts make a good drainage base for houseplants.

254. A few mothballs in the soil will keep cats out of potted plants.

255. Film canisters (35mm) make great containers for small parts, matches, coins, and other camping or travel necessities.

256. A damp sponge dipped in baking soda makes a good insect remover when cleaning your car.

257. A couple of slit sections of an old garden hose make a good set of handles for a pane of glass.

258. Follow label directions.

259. Use all the colors in the rainbow.

260. Cut the bottom off a plastic milk jug to make a handy funnel.

261. Chlorine bleach will clear mold and mildew from bathtubs and showers.

262. Alcohol will neutralize the sting and burn after handling hot peppers.

263. Tack a carpenter's apron to the top of a wooden step ladder for a neat place to hold tools.

264. Wood ashes are a good repellent for slugs and snails.

265. A couple of tablespoons of baking soda in the bathwater will "soften" and "brighten" the pet's coat.

266. A paste of baking soda and water will ease the pain from bee stings.

267. Banana peels are an excellent source of phosphorus and potassium for the garden.

268. A couple of sticks of chalk in a toolbox reduce moisture and prevent rust.

269. Beer is a great marinade for inexpensive cuts of meat.

270. Save the adult beverage until the work is done.

271. Cover the open end of your vacuum with cheesecloth and use it to remove dust from a drawer filled with small objects.

272. Used sheets of fabric softener make great dust removers for TV and computer screens.

273. Large plastic garbage bags make great disposable aprons.

274. Slit a section of old hose and use it as a blade protector for saws, axes, and other cutting tools.

275. Cat litter is a good absorber for spills on the garage floor.

276. A couple drops of chlorine bleach in a humidifier prevent bacterial growth.

277. To clean and deodorize your cutting board, rub a lemon rind over it.

278. Pipe cleaners make great twist ties for garbage bags.

279. A mixture of cornstarch, ammonia, and water makes a good window cleaner.

280. Sprinkle cornstarch inside rubber gloves to make them easier to put on and take off.

281. Place a cotton ball saturated with your favorite fragrance in the bag of your vacuum cleaner.

282. Lay an open stepladder on its side to make a great sawhorse.

283. Lemon juice combined with salt removes most fruit stains from your hands.

284. Salt sprinkled on soap suds will reduce them.

285. Aluminum foil mulch keeps aphids away from tomato plants.

286. Use your local hardware store as a resource.

287. One last thing: Read the instructions.

Other Handyman Resources

Carrell, A. (1990). *Best home hints from the super handyman*. Dallas Tx: Taylor Publishing Co.

Reader's Digest. (1995). *The family handyman: Helpful hints*. Pleasantville, NY: The Reader's Digest Association.

Reader's Digest. (1991). *Practical problem solver*. Pleasantville, NY: The Reader's Digest Association.

Reader's Digest. (1988). *Household hints and handy tips*. Pleasantville, NY: The Reader's Digest Association.